HANDBOOK OF CRIBBAGE

*Containing Full Directions for Playing All the
Varieties of The Game and The Laws
Which Govern Them*

by

William Brisbane Dick

New York—1885

CONTENTS

INTRODUCTION 1

SIX-CARD CRIBBAGE 3
Dealing,
Laying Out for Crib,
Cutting For The Start, Playing,
Example of Playing,
Playing Last-Cards,
Counts and Combinations in Play,
Showing the Hands, Scoring,
Hints on the Crib and Play,
Playing to the Score,
Long Sequences in Play

THE VALUE OF HAND 21
Counting on the Value of Hands

FIVE-CARD CRIBBAGE 35
Instructive Example,
Three-Handed Cribbage

FOUR-HANDED CRIBBAGE 40
Hints on Playing,
Long Sequences in Play,
A Remarkable Problem

LAWS OF CRIBBAGE 47
Cutting, Shuffling and Dealing,
Laying Out, Playing,
Showing and Scoring

HANDBOOK OF CRIBBAGE.

INTRODUCTION

Of the origin of Cribbage we are not aware that anything is known further than that it is essentially an English game.

The game of Cribbage is entirely distinct and different from all other card-games. The method of playing it, and the constant variety of combinations which present themselves, render it one of the most interesting and fascinating games.

To those who have become familiar with, and have mastered the characteristic peculiarities of the game, it offers an attractive pastime, requiring only an occasional moment of transient mental effort, and leaving the players ample opportunity for social intercourse. The game is played with a full pack of fifty-two cards: Sixty-one points constitutes the game. These points are scored on a Cribbage Board, of which a representation is here given. It consists of two longitudinal divisions, one division for each player's independent score. Each division contains sixty holes; and at one end, between the divisions, is another hole, called the " game-hole," which is common to both, making each sixty-one points. For convenience in scoring, each division is marked off in subdivisions of five points each.

The board is placed either across or lengthways between the players. It is a matter of indifference how the board is placed; but the count must commence from that end which contains the sixty-first, or game-hole; beginning at the outside edge (A or B), and passing along it to the top, then down the inside row to game. (See Diagram below)

Four pegs (of which each player uses two), are used for scoring.

Scoring is done by advancing the lower peg and counting the points ahead of the front peg. Like a horse race, this movement of pegs will lead the winning player to the sixty-first, or game-hole.

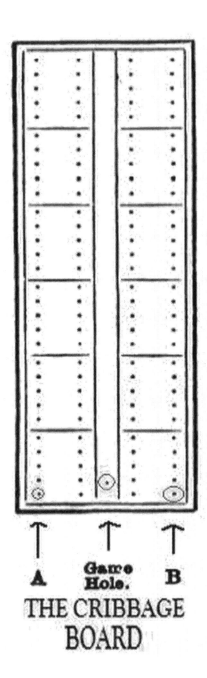

A Game Hole. B

THE CRIBBAGE BOARD

SIX-CARD CRIBBAGE.

Six-Card Cribbage is much more popular in this country than any of the other Cribbage games; and should, therefore, be first considered.

DEALING.

The players having cut for deal (*See* Laws 1 to 5,) the pack is shuffled, and the non-dealer cuts it. The dealer re-unites the packets and gives six cards to each player, by one at a time, commencing with his adversary. The undealt portion of the pack is placed face downwards, between the game-hole end of the board and the edge of the table.

LAYING OUT FOR CRIB.

The deal being completed, the players proceed to look at their hands and to *lay out for crib.* Each has to put out two cards. The players, having decided which two cards they deem it expedient to discard, place the discarded cards face downwards on the table, by the side of the board nearest to the dealer. The two cards last put out are placed on the top of the two first put out.

The four cards laid out are called the *crib.*

CUTTING FOR THE START.

After the crib is laid out, the non-dealer cuts the pack and the dealer turns up the top card of the packet left by his adversary. The card turned up is called the *start.*

The packets of the cut are now re-united, and the dealer places the start face upwards upon the pack.

If the start is a Knave the dealer marks two (called *two for his heels).*

PLAYING.

The hands are now played in the following manner:—The non-dealer plays any card from his hand he thinks fit, placing it face upwards on the table by the side of the board nearest to himself, and calls out the number at which it is valued.

The King, Queen, Knave, and Ten (called *Tenth cards)* are valued at ten each, the other cards at the number of pips on them.

The dealer then plays any card he thinks fit, placing it face upwards by his side of the board, and calls out the value' of his card added to the value of the card first played.

The non-dealer next plays another card, and then the dealer, and so on, as long as any cards remain in hand, or until a card cannot be played without passing the number thirty-one.

When it happens that a player cannot play without passing thirty-one, he says " go." His adversary then, if he has a card which will *come-in, i. e.,* which can be played without passing thirty-one, is entitled to, and must, play it.

When a player has no card in hand that will make thirty-one or under, he says " go;" but his opponent must continue to play if he can mark the point for the " go." Thus: Suppose the play has reached twenty-six; the next player having no card less than a Six, therefore, says "go." His opponent having a Two and an Ace; must play them both, before he can score one for the *go.*

When there is a "go," the player, whose card last played comes nearest to thirty-one, makes the " go," and marks one point. If, however, the player makes exactly thirty-one, he marks two points, for the thirty-one, instead of one for the "go."

As soon as thirty-one, or the number nearest to it is made in playing the hand, the cards already played should be turned down, so that no confusion may arise by their being mixed with the succeeding cards.

When the hands have been played out, the player who played the last card marks one for " last card."

The hands and crib are then displayed, reckoned, and the points marked ; each party making use of the start-card (or turn-up) as if it were a portion of his hand.

The non-dealer has the first show. He reckons the number of points contained in his hand, with the aid of the start-card, and marks it to his score in the game. The dealer then shows his hand, in the same manner, also including the start-card in his reckoning, and marks the points gained.

Lastly, the dealer counts the points in his crib, still using the start-card as part of it, and marks the points to his score.

If neither party has marked sufficient points to win the game, another deal is made; and, if needed, another, and still another, until one of the players has marked sixty-one points, and wins the game.

As soon as sixty-one is reached, the game ends, and all play ceases for that game.

The number of points constituting a game is in many instances fixed at one hundred and twenty-one, but this should he settled before commencing to play.

EXAMPLE OF PLAYING.

Let us suppose A and B sitting down to play Six-card Cribbage, and by following out their first hand, the mode of playing the game will be learned at once:—

A, being dealer, deals six cards to each, one at a time, the Cribbage-board being placed for counting in the usual way between them.

Having made the deal, each player discards two cards for the crib, and the start-card being cut, and turned, the play begins; the hand of each consisting obviously of four cards.

B leads (suppose) a King, and says, " ten."

A answers with a Five, and says "fifteen," and marks two for it.

B rejoins with another King, saying, " twenty-five."

A plays a Six, and marks two points for making thirty-one.

Each player now turns face downwards the cards he has so far played.

B continues the play putting down a Nine, and says " nine."

A follows with an Eight, saying, "seventeen."

B answers with a Ten, and marks three points for the sequence of three cards, composed of the Eight, Nine, and Ten. He calls at the same time, "twenty- seven."

A's last card being a Five, he cannot come in under thirty-one, and therefore declares it to be " a go," on which B take another point for the *go.*

The cards are now all played out, with the exception of A's solitary Five, which he throws down, and marks one for the *last card.*

The hands and crib are then reckoned, and scored, each party making similar use of the start or turn-up card. Another deal is made, and passes alternately, until victory is proclaimed by the conqueror's attaining the sixty-first, or game-hole.

PLAYING LAST CARDS.

As all the cards must be played out, should one party have exhausted his hand, and his adversary have yet two cards, the latter are to be played, and, should they yield any advantage, it must be taken. For instance: C has played out his four cards, and D having two left (an Eight and Seven), calls fifteen, as he throws them down, and marks three points—two for the fifteen and one for the last card.

Again, should D's two cards have been a pair (Threes, for instance), he marks two for the pair, and a third point for the last card.

Speculating on this and other probabilities, it is always advisable to endeavor, when last player, to retain as close cards as possible, for this -will frequently make three or four additional points. But this demands further illustration, as it is of paramount importance. For example:

Suppose you hold for the last two cards a Seven and Eight, and that your adversary has only one card remaining in his hand, the probable chance of its being either a Six or a Nine (in either of which cases you come in for four points) is eleven to two; therefore, it is only eleven to two, against gaining three points by this play, exclusive of the " last card;" whereas, were you to retain, as your last two cards, a Seven with a Ten, or any two cards similarly wide apart, you have no chance to score more for them than the "last card," as there is no probability of their coming in for any sequence ; or, if you can retain a pair of any kind for the last two cards (your adversary having only one card, and he being the first player), you by this means make a certainty of two points, exclusive of the "last card." By the same rule you ought always to retain such cards as will (supposing your adversary to have none left) make a pair, fifteen, &c; for by this means you may gain many points which you otherwise could not possibly get.

COUNTS AND COMBINATIONS IN PLAY.

During the play of the hand the players are entitled to score for certain combinations of cards as follows:—pairs, fifteen, sequences, the go, and thirty-one.

Pairs.—If, when a card is played, the next card played pairs it (for instance, if a four is played to a four), the player pairing is entitled to mark two points.

Pair Royal.—If, after a pair has been played, the card next played is also of the same denomination, *a, pair royal* is made, which entitles the player making it to mark six points.

Double Pair Royal.— If, after a *pair royal* has been played, the card next played is again of the same kind, it constitutes a *double pair royal* which entitles the player to a score of twelve points, in addition to the pair already scored by him.

Tenth cards only pair with Tenth cards of the same denomination. Thus: Kings pair with Kings, Queens with Queens, and so on; but Kings do not pair with Queens, Knaves, or Tens, although they are all Tenth cards.

Fifteen.—If during the play of the hand a player reaches exactly fifteen, by reckoning the pips of all the played cards, he is entitled to mark two points. Thus: a Nine is first led; the second player plays a Six; he calls fifteen and marks two.

Sequences.—The sequence of the cards is King, Queen, Knave, Ten, Nine, Eight, Seven, Six, Five, Four, Three, Two, Ace. The Ace is not in sequence with the King and Queen. The King, Queen, Knave, and Ten, though they each count ten towards thirty-one in play, reckon in sequences in the above order. Thus: Knave, Ten, Nine are in sequence.

If any three cards, played consecutively, are such that any arrangement of them will form a sequence the player of the third card is entitled to mark three (called a *run* of three).

If a fourth card is similarly played, the player of it is entitled to a run of four; if a fifth card is similarly played, a run of five accrues, and so on.

If there is a break in the sequence, and in the subsequent play, the break is filled up, without the intervention of a card out of sequence order, the player completing the sequence is entitled to a score of one for each card forming the sequence.

For example : A plays a Four; B plays a Three; if A follows with a Two or a Five, he is entitled to a run of three. Suppose A plays a Two; if B now plays an Ace or a Five, he gains a run of four, or, if he plays a Four, he gains a run of three, and so on, as long as either player plays a card that will *come in.*

It is not necessary that the cards forming a sequence should be played in order. Thus: A plays a Four; B a Two: A a Five. B can then come in with a Three, and mark a run of two, three, four, Ave. After the Three is played, A can come in with an Ace or a Six, making a run of five, or with a Four, making a run of four. But if any card not in sequence intervenes, the run is stopped. Thus: if Four, Two, Five, and Five are played in this order, a Three or a Six will not come in, as the second Five, which intervenes, forms no part of the run.

Again: suppose the cards played in this order: Four, Two, Three, One, Five, Two, Four, One; the third card entitles the run of three; the fourth to a run of four; the fifth to a run of five. The sixth card, the Two, has no run, as the second card (another Two) intervenes, and the Four is wanting to complete the sequence. The seventh card takes a run of five; and the last card has no run, as the Ace previously played blocks the Three.

Again: suppose the cards played in this order: One, Five, Six, Three, Two, Four:—there is no ran until the Four is played. The Four completes the sequence, and entitles to a run of six.

The Go.—The player who approaches most nearly to thirty-one, during the play of the hand is entitled to mark one, for the *last card, go,* or *end hole.* If a player reaches thirty-one exactly, he marks two instead of one.

For instance: two Tenth cards and a Four are played, making twenty-four. If the next player has no card in hand under an Eight, he cannot come in, and his adversary marks a *go.* If, however, the adversary has a Seven, he may play that and score two for thirty-one, instead of one for the go; or, if he has a Four he may play it, when he marks two for the pair, and, if his adversary has no card that will come *in (i. e.,* no card under a Pour remaining in his hand), the last player marks one for the *go.*

Compound Scores.—It not unfrequently happens that more than one score can be reckoned at the same time. Thus, in the case last given, a pair and a go are scored together. So also a pair and a thirty-one, or a pair and a fifteen, may be reckoned together—scoring four; or a sequence and a fifteen (for example—Four, Five, Six are played), scoring five, and so on, with other combinations.

SHOWING.

Last Card.—When all the cards have been played, the player who played the last card marks one point for " last card." This supersedes the " go," as no player can say " go " unless he has a card or cards in his hand, and which he finds will not come in without exceeding thirty-one.

As soon as the last card is played, the players *show* their hands, and reckon aloud for certain combinations of cards in them. The non-dealer has the *first show.* He places his hand face upwards on the table, and reckons and marks the points in it, making use of the *start as* though it were a part of his hand, but without mixing it with his cards.

The dealer then shows his hand, and similarly reckons it aloud, and marks the points in it and the *start* combined. He then shows the crib, and reckons aloud, and marks the points made with it and the *start.*

The points counted in hand or crib may be made by fifteens, by pairs or pairs royal, by sequences, by flushes, or by his nob.

Fifteens in hand or crib are counted by adding together all the different cards (including the *start),* the pips of which will make exactly fifteen, without counting the same set of cards twice over. In reckoning fifteens, Tenth cards are valued at ten each.

Each separate fifteen that can be made with a different combination reckons two. For example: a player holding, either with or without the *start,* a Tenth card and a Five, reckons Two, or as it is called *fifteen-two.* If he has another Five, he combines this also with the Tenth card and reckons two more, or *fifteen-four.*

Suppose a player holds two Tenth cards, a Four, with a Five, and a Five is turned up, he reckons fifteen-eight, the combination being as follows:

Ten of Clubs	Ten of Spades
Five of Clubs	Five of Spades
Ten of Clubs	Ten of Spades
Five of Spades	Five of Clubs

In this instance, the Four does not assist in the count, and is, therefore, what is called an *indifferent card.*

Again, a Nine, an indifferent card, and three Threes give three different combinations of fifteen, each of which reckons two. Thus:—

Nine of Spades	Nine of Spades
Three of Hearts	Three of Hearts
Three of Clubs	Three of Diamonds

Nine of Spades.
Three of Clubs
Three of Diamonds

and so on for other cards.

Pairs are reckoned on the same principle as when playing the hand. In the example last but one the total score would be twelve, viz : eight for the fifteens, and four for the two pairs; in the last example, six for the pair royal would have to be added to the six for the fifteens.

To take a less easy example, a hand consisting of four Fives, and an indifferent card, would score twenty (twelve for the double pair royal and eight for the fifteens), as under:—

Five of Spades Five of Hearts Five of Clubs	Five of Spades Five of Hearts Five of Diamonds
Five of Spades Five of Clubs Five of Diamonds	Five of Hearts Five of Clubs Five of Diamonds.

It will be observed that these are all the fifteens which can be made without reckoning the same set of three cards together more than once.

Suppose the four Fives to be held in hand and the start to be any Tenth card, then the score would be eight points more, making twenty-eight points in all.

Sequences of three or more cards are counted as in the play of the hand, but with this addition, that, if one card of a sequence can be substituted for another of the same kind, the sequence is reckoned again. Thus, a Seven, Eight and two 1*0168 give two sequences of seven, eight, nine, by substituting one Nine for the other, in addition to the fifteen and the pair, making the total ten.

Suppose the hand or crib to consist of two Tens, two Nines, and an Eight. Here are four sequences of three cards each, viz:

Ten of Clubs Nine of Hearts Eight of Spades	Ten of Clubs Nine of Spades Eight of Spades
Ten of Diamonds Nine of Hearts Eight of Spades	Ten of Diamonds Nine of Spades Eight of Spades

These count twelve in addition to the two pairs, which make the total sixteen.

To take a more difficult example—the hand or crib, (including the start) contains Six, Seven,

Seven, Eight, Eight. This hand is counted thus : four-fifteens (eight), two pairs (four), four sequences of three each (twelve), in all twenty-four.

A Flush, is reckoned by a player whose hand consists of four cards of the same suit. The flush counts four; if the start is of the same suit as the hand, the flush counts five. For example: a player has Two, Three, Pour, Five of the same suit, and a Six is turned up. The hand counts fifteen-four; five for sequence, nine; and four for the flush, thirteen. If the start is also of the same suit, the hand reckons fourteen. No flush can be counted in crib, unless the start is of the same suit as the crib, when the flush reckons five.

His Nob.—If a player holds in hand or crib, the Knave of the suit turned up, he counts *one for his nob.*

When the hands and crib are reckoned, the deal is at an end. The cards are put together and shuffled, and a fresh deal commences. The player who was the non-dealer in the first hand now deals, and so on, alternately, until the game is won.

The foregoing examples are sufficient for the present, to illustrate the various ways in which cards may be combined and counted at Cribbage.

In another part of this work we will more thoroughly investigate the most important combinations that may be made with five cards.

SCORING.

The points made during the hand accrue in the following order: two for his heels; points in the play of the hand to the player gaining them as they are made; the non-dealer's show; the dealer's show, and the crib show.

The game is sixty-one up; (or, may be, by previous agreement, one hundred and twenty-one, being *twice round* the board). Each player marks the points to which he is entitled as soon as they accrue, by placing a peg in the hole on the board corresponding to the number to which he is entitled. For the first score on each side, only one peg is used; for the second score, the second peg (called the *foremost peg)* is placed the requisite number of holes in front of the first. At the next score the *hindmost peg* is moved in front of the other, and becomes in its turn the foremost peg. By marking in this way, the adversary is enabled to check each score, as the number of holes between each peg shows whether the score is correctly marked.

The players first mark *up the hoard,* commencing from the game-hole end, each using the row of holes on the outer edge of the board, and nearest to himself. When a player arrives at the top, he proceeds to mark *down the board,* on the inner row ef holes on his side of the board. The player who first scores sixty-one (or one hundred and twenty-one, as the case may be), wins the game. When the game is won, the winner places his foremost peg in the game-hole.

If a player wins the game before his adversary has scored thirty-one (or Sixty-one, if twice round be played) points, he wins a double, or " lurch " (*see* Law 34).

HINTS ON LAYING OUT FOR CRIB, AND PLAYING.

1. In laying out for crib, it is necessary to bear in mind whether it is your deal or your adversary's. When you are the dealer, you should lay out cards that are likely to score in crib; when you are not the dealer, you should do precisely the reverse, laying out bad cards for the adversary's crib (called *baulking the crib).*

2. The least likely card to reckon in crib is a King, as that card can only score in sequence one way. For a similar reason, an Ace is a good baulk.

The best baulking cards for the opponent's crib are King, with either Ten, Nine, Eight, Seven, Six, or Ace, (King, Nine being the best); or Queen, with any of these except the Ten.

If unable to lay out any such combination, discard cards that are not in sequence nor near together.

Wide *even* cards are good baulks, even cards being less likely to give a score than *odd* ones, or than one even and one odd one.

If you have the choice between two cards of the same suit, or of different suits, prefer the latter, so as not to give a chance of a flush in crib.

3. The best cards to put out for your own crib (and, therefore, those to be avoided for your adversary's) are Fives, Five and Six, Five and a Tenth card, Three and Two, Seven and Eight, Four and One, Nine and Six, or pairs, particularly low pairs. If unable to lay out any of these, discard as close cards as possible.

It is generally good play to retain a sequence in hand, as, if a card similar to any one of the cards held is turned up, it gives you eight in hand at least. Pairs royal are also good cards to keep.

The rule to keep these and sequences in your hand also applies when discarding for the adversary's crib, unless the two other cards are in the list just mentioned. For example: with Queen, Knave, Ten, Nine, Four, Ace, you should put out the Four and Ace, for your own crib; but for your adversary's the Queen and Nine, keeping a fifteen and sacrificing the sequence. The Queen and Nine are chosen because they are the widest apart; also, retaining the Knave gives a chance for " one for his nob."

4. The lay-out is affected by the state of the score. Towards the end of the game, if you have cards that in all probability will take you out, the consideration of baulking the opponent's crib is of but little consequence.

5. In playing the cards, the card first to be chosen should be the one that presents the least chance of an adverse score. Aces, Twos, Threes, or Fours, are the best cards to lead, as no fifteen can be made

from them, and the only chance of a score is by pairing them. The pair, however, is very likely to be declined, as it is commonly the game to begin with a card of which you hold a duplicate (except with two Fives), so that you may make a pair royal if paired.

Also, if an Ace, Two, Three, or Four, is led, the second player *must* play a card which makes less than fifteen, giving you the chance of making fifteen; especially if with Ace and Four, or Two and Three, if you have led one of them, then the play of any tenth card (of which there are sixteen in the pack) will enable you to make fifteen.

Also, with Nine and Three, or Four and Seven, if the Three or the Four is led and paired, the Nine or Seven makes fifteen.

And further, if the second hand plays a Tenth card to the low one first led, you have a chance of a *safe pair, i. e.,* of pairing with so high a card that a pair royal cannot be made without taking the adversary beyond thirty-one.

6. When leading from a sequence, the highest or lowest is to be chosen in preference to the middle card.

7. If the adversary plays a close card to the one led, it is frequently because he desires you to make a run of three, he lying with a fourth card that will come in. Whether you should accept the run, or decline it by playing wide, depends on the state of the game. *{See* Hint 10.)

8. If the adversary plays a card which you can pair, or make fifteen of, choose the latter. At the same time you must not forget, if a Seven or Eight is led, and you make fifteen, that you give the opponent a chance of coming in with a Six or a Nine for a sequence.

9. Avoid making eleven with a Four, as, if the Four is paired, the adversary gains four holes. The rules applies to all similar combinations. For example: twelve made with a Three, twenty-seven made with a Four, or twenty-eight with a Three.

Avoid making the number twenty-one in play, as then a Tenth card comes in for two points.

10. When playing the cards, the state of the score should constantly be considered.

When you are ahead in the game, or have your average, you should endeavor to keep the advantage by playing wide cards, by refusing pairs, or by declining to make fifteen with close cards. Playing in this way is called *playing off.* On the other hand, if you are behind in the game, you should run risks to get on, as by pairing (risking a pair royal), by making fifteen with close- cards, or by playing close cards, when, if your adversary makes a small run, you have a card that will come in and give you a larger one. Playing in this way is called *playing on.*

11. When you are safe at home, the rule respecting sequences *(See Hint 3)* does not always apply, especially with sequences containing Seven and Eight. It is then frequently the game to hold a wide card, to enable you to play off. Again, when near the end of the game, and you want to make points in play, in order to play out, you should endeavor to hold two low cards and one high one.

12. In reckoning the hand and crib, it will assist the novice to keep to a regular order. He should first search his cards for fifteens, then for pairs, then for sequences, then for a flush, and lastly, for his nob.

13. At Six-card Cribbage there is not so strong a reason for baulking the crib as at Five-card Cribbage. The average scores are larger at the Six-card game.

The non-dealer is at home at the end of the first hand if he scores twelve, the dealer if he scores seventeen.

At the end of the second deal each player is at home at twenty-nine holes.

In the first deal it is a considerable advantage to either player to exceed his average, and, consequently, both should *play on;* but when a player sees he cannot get home in the first deal, he should commence by *playing off.*

With only high cards in hand, it is advisable to keep two cards that will score in play (for instance, a Seven and an Eight), so that if your adversary is obliged to play a card more than you, you come in for a score at the end of the hand.

PLAYING TO THE STATE OF THE SCORE.

In Six-card Cribbage, the number of points in a hand would average seven, and in the crib, five.

The average number of points to be made each time by play is from four to five. The dealer has the advantage here, because he plays last.

According to Pasquin*, a player is only entitled to twenty-five points for three shows and play, and the dealer is at home, if, when he has played his second deal, he is twenty-five points up the board, and when he has dealt for the third time, within eleven holes of game. This calculation is now considered erroneous.

The modern system of calculation is to allow twenty-nine instead of twenty-five holes for the three shows, and to consider that at the end of the second round each player is at home at twenty-nine holes.

As you are on a parity at starting, being both at home, you will play your first hand with moderate caution, making fair risks, but not running into too wide speculation.

On taking up your second hand, you will adapt your play to the relative scores on the board, and will play *on* or *off,* according to the dictates of policy.

The same rules will govern your conduct during the remainder of the game; and should your adversary have gained the preference, or should you be more than home, both cases must be taken into consideration in playing your hand.

---

* 'A Treatise on the Game of Cribbage,' London, 1791, 12 mo; 2nd edit., corrected, 1807, by Anthony Pasquin [pseudonym for John William (1761-1818)]

If your cards present a flattering prospect, and you are by no means home, it is your duty to make a push, in order to regain the lead by running ; whereas, should your adversary be ahead of you, and should you take up bad cards, it will be the best play to keep off, and only endeavor to stop your antagonist as much as possible, and thereby have less probable chance of closing the game, through his not being able to make his points good.

LONG SEQUENCES IN PLAY.

As so many points are to be gained in play by the formation of long sequences, you will frequently find it advantageous, having eligible cards for the purpose in view, to lead or play so as to tempt your adversary to form a short sequence, in order that you may come in for a longer. And this opportunity is particularly to be sought for, when a few holes are essential to your game though gained at any risk.

The tyro may find it difficult to reckon the long sequences that frequently occur in the course of play. We give, therefore, the following example:

A and B are playing Six-card Cribbage.

A leads a Four.

B plays a Two.

A responds with a Three, and scores three for the sequences of three cards.

B plays an Ace, and scores four for the sequence of four cards.

A replies with a Two, and scores three for the sequence formed by the last three cards, viz: the Ace, Two, and Three.

B rejoins with a Four, and scores four for the last four cards played.

Observe, that the Four and Two originally played do not form any part of the last sequence; also, that the aggregate number of pips played is sixteen.

A now plays a Five, which forms a sequence of five, yielding a score of five.

The aggregate number of pips played is now twenty-one.

B holds the last card, which, fortunately for him, is a Three. This forms a sequence of five, which, together with one for last card, gives B an additional score of six. Observe, that the last sequence is composed of the last five cards played, and is formed without including either of the first three cards played.

Many other examples might be given, but for our purpose the above is sufficient.

The longest sequence that can arise in play is one of seven cards, viz., Ace, Two, Three, Four, Five, Six and Seven. If the Eight were added to the above the number of pips would exceed thirty-one.

THE VALUE OF HANDS.

ON COUNTING THE VALUE OF HANDS.

Under the heading of " Showing," we have already said something about the various counts and combinations of .the different Cribbage hands, but it is necessary to examine this important matter in detail in order to arrive at a more thorough knowledge of the subject.

The difficulties attendant on counting correctly, on all occasions, whether hand or crib, will soon vanish before attention and practice. Take a pack of cards and deal out a number of hands in detail. Examine these hands and reckon up the number of points they would yield, if held at Cribbage; lifting a start-card to be combined with them. The principal difficulties of reckoning will be found to arise from the several ways in which fifteens and sequences (the latter more especially) may be computed. The summing up the value of pairs, pairs-royal, etc., on the other hand, is very simple.

To reckon correctly the amount of the four cards of which a hand is originally composed, would be sufficiently easy, were it not for the subsequent introduction of the *start* card, which though useless in play, counts, at the end of the deal, as a part of the hand.

We will now examine a few cases of counting shaped in the form of questions to which we call the attention of the student.

First Question.—How many points must be taken for a hand of cards, composed of the King of hearts, Six of spades, Four of diamonds, Two of spades, with Eight of diamonds turned up ?

Answer.—None! There not being among the five cards combined as above, either pairs, sequences, flushes, or fifteens; consequently, the hand is altogether worthless.

Second Question.—In the last example, suppose that, instead of the Eight of diamonds, the Five of spades had been the card turned up. In such case, how many points might then be marked for the hand ?

Answer.—Seven; and they are to be counted as follows:—The Four, Five, and Six, being added together, make fifteen-two. The King and Five form a second fifteen, making four. Then the Four, Five, and Six make a sequence of three, and the addition of these three points, makes an aggregate number of seven.

Third Question.—How many points may be marked for a hand comprising the Six, Seven, Eight, and Nine of spades; supposing the Seven of hearts to be the start card!

Answer.—Twenty; and the points are reckoned in the following manner: —

The Seven and Eight of spades make one fifteen (8 and *7*), which gives: **2**

The Eight of spades and Seven of hearts make a second fifteen: **2**

The Nine and Six of spades make a third fifteen: **2**

The Six, Seven, Eight and Nine of spades form a sequence of four cards; for which four is counted: **4**

The Six, Eight and Nine of Spades, with the Seven of hearts, form a sequence of four more: **4**

The Six, Seven, Eight and Nine of spades, being all of the same suit, count four: **4**

Lastly, the two Sevens form a pair of Sevens, giving: **2**

Adding the total number of points from above we get a sum of: **20**

The student is requested to examine this example ; and to carefully observe the manner in which, the sequences are formed by placing the same cards in different combinations.

Fourth Question.— How many points should be marked for a hand, or crib containing the Five of clubs, the Five of spades, the Five of diamonds, and the Knave of hearts, with the Five of hearts turned up ?

Answer.—We have already shown, that a hand consisting of four Fives with any Tenth card turned up for the start will count twenty-eight points. In the hand under consideration, however, the player holds the Knave of the same suit as the start card and therefore reckons "one for his Nob," making the total number of points, twenty-nine, the greatest number that can be marked for any single hand or crib. Thus :— The Knave and Five of spades make fifteen,

which gives two points: **2**

The Knave and Five of diamonds, ditto: **2**

The Knave and Five of clubs, ditto: **2**

The Knave and Five of hearts, ditto: **2**

The Five of spades, Five of diamonds, and Five of clubs, being three fives, make also fifteen: **2**

The Five of spades, Five of diamonds, and Five of hearts, ditto: **2**

The Five of spades, Five of hearts, and Five of clubs: **2**

The Five of diamonds, Five of hearts, and Five of clubs: **2**

The double pair-royal, composed of four Fives: **12**

One point for the Knave, being of the same suit as the card turned up: **1**

Adding the total number of points from above we get a sum of: **29**

The foregoing example is useful in showing how fifteens may be formed. The same cards are not reckoned together more than once in each combination ; but by slightly altering the arrangement each time, the changes are rung over and over again.

Fifth. Question.—Supposing a hand or crib to consist of two Kings, a Queen, and a Knave, with a second Queen turned up for the start,—how many points may be marked?

Answer.—Sixteen. All the cards being Tenth cards it is clear no fifteens can be counted; but, by forming different combinations, the hand may be made to yield four distinct sequences .of three cards each, which, when united, count twelve. Four additional points are obtained for the two pairs, making the total number sixteen points.

"We purposely refrain from giving the particulars of this count in detail. By selecting from the pack the cards which comprise the hand, the student will find little difficulty in working out the different combinations that may be formed.

Sixth Question.—Supposing a hand to be composed of two Sevens, an Eight, and an Ace; and an Eight be turned for the start-card—how many can be marked for this hand 1

Answer.—Fourteen; ten points being made by five fifteens, and the remaining four by the two pairs of Sevens and Eights.

Observe:—That each Eight reckons with each Seven for fifteen, and the two Sevens with the Ace make another fifteen.

Seventh Question.—Supposing a hand to consist of two Sixes and two Fives, and a Four be turned for a start-card; how many points can be marked for such a hand f

Answer.—Twenty-four. Eight points for the four fifteens; twelve points for the four sequences of three cards each; and four points for the two pairs,—making a total of twenty-four points.

Eighth Question.—Supposing a hand to be composed of a Two, two Threes, and a Four; making eight points for the two sequences and the pair,—what start card may be turned that will afford no additional advantage to the hand ?

Answer.— *None,* for whatever card is turned, the hand will be improved. Any card from the Ace to the Five, inclusive, may be employed to form new sequences. A Six will make fifteens. A Seven will make a fifteen by being combined with the two Threes and the Two. An Eight will make two fifteens when combined with each of two Threes and the Four. A Nine with the pair of Threes reckons fifteen. Any Tenth card, when combined with the Threes and the Two, will form fifteens.

We will now proceed to illustrate how a Double Pair-Royal, when combined with another favorable card, may be reckoned. Such a hand is easily counted when spread on the table in the form of a square, with the single card in the centre of the Double-Pair Royal.

The following examples will explain what we mean:—

No. 1.	No. 2.
8 8	9 9
7	6
8 8	9 9

No. 3.	No. 4.
10 10	7 7
5	8
10 10	7 7

The value of either of the above four hands is twenty points. Twelve for the Double Pair Royal, and eight for the four fifteens, which are formed by combining the centre card successively with each of the four by which it is surrounded.

No. 5.		No. 6.	
7	7	3	3
1		9	
7	7	3	3

No. 7.		No. 8.	
6	6	4	4
3		7	
6	6	4	4

The above four hands count twenty-four points each—Twelve for the Double Pair-Royal, and twelve more for the six fifteens which may be successively formed by combining the centre card with two of the other four, first around the four sides of the square, and then twice diagonally.

We have already shown how the highest two hands—twenty-eight, and twenty-nine points— may be held and counted. We now glance at the other hands which may be held at Cribbage, descending from these two greater hands, to those of lower rank.

The combinations and their values given in the following examples, are confined to those in which *all* the five cards combine to make the score. Those combinations into which only four, three or two of the five cards enter, leaving the others useless as far as reckoning is concerned, are so numerous that it would be almost impossible to enumerate them; but they are much easier to comprehend, as they involve fewer cards.

The Numbers Twenty-seven, Twenty-six and Twenty-five cannot be made by any combination of the cards.

The Number Twenty-four may occur in a hand in a variety of ways. In addition to the instances, just quoted, in which twenty-four is made by a Double Pair-Royal and a fifth favorable card, the following examples are worthy of notice. Each hand, it will be observed, is composed of two close pairs and a close single card. As it does not matter which of the five cards we assume to have been turned up for the start, it will be more convenient and simple to place the whole five cards together without distinction.

$$4\ 4\ 5\ 5\ 6 \qquad\qquad 4\ 5\ 5\ 6\ 6$$
$$7\ 7\ 8\ 8\ 9 \qquad\qquad 4\ 4\ 5\ 6\ 6$$

Observe:—That there can be no flush in a hand or crib of twenty-four, pairs being necessary to its formation.

The Number Twenty-three occurs but rarely; three Fives combined with, a Six and a Four produce a hand or crib of twenty-three. This hand may also be formed by a combination of three Fives and a pair of Knaves; the start-card turned up being a Five of the same suit as one of the Knaves.

The Number Twenty-two is produced by the union of three Fives with a pair of Kings, Queens, &c. The last fifteen made up by the three Fives themselves, is frequently overlooked by inexperienced players.

The Number Twenty-one requires a few examples. Either one of the six following hands forms twenty-one.

```
  3 3 3 4 5              6 7 7 7 8
  4 4 4 5 6              8 8 8 6 7
  6 6 6 4 5              7 7 7 8 9
```

Twenty-one may also be formed by a combination of three Fives and two Tenth cards, one of them being a Knave, and the start turned up being a Five of the same suit as the Knave.

The Number Twenty is not of uncommon occurrence. We give the following examples:

```
  3  3  4  4  5 ,        6  6  8  8  7
  3  3  5  5. 4.         7  7  7  1  1
  3  3  3  9  9          7  7  7  8  8
  4  4  4  7  7          8  8  8  7  7
  6  6  6  3  3          9  9  9  6  6
  6  6  6  9  9         10 10 10  5  5
```

Each of the above ten hands reckons twenty points.

Twenty may also be formed with the assistance of a flush. (See example in *Third Question*.)

The Number Nineteen cannot be made by any possible combination of the cards which compose a hand or crib.

The Number Eighteen is exemplified in the following cases:—

```
  2 2 3 4 4              6 6 6 9 3
  3 3 3 6 6              7 7 7 1 8
```

The manner in which an Ace may be combined with three sevens, as shown in the last of the above examples, is worthy of notice, being a combination that is frequently overlooked by beginners.

The Number Seventeen is usually composed of cards analogous to those shown in the following examples:—

3 3 3 2 4	4 4 4 3 5
4 4 4 2 3	5 5 5 3 4
6 6 6 7 8	5 5 5 6 7

Seventeen may also be formed exclusively with Tenth cards, thus:— two Queens, two Kings, and a Knave of the same suit as the card turned for the start. A *flush* of Six, Seven, Eight, and Ace; with another Ace turned for the start card also reckons seventeen.

The Number Sixteen is not of unfrequent occurrence. We append a variety of examples:—

1 1 2 3 3	1 2 2 3 3
1 2 3 3 2	1 1 2 2 3
1 1 3 3 2	2 2 3 3 4
3 3 3 6 9	2 3 3 4 4
3 4 5 5 4	3 4 5 6 6
4 4 5 6 7	4 5 6 6 9
4 5 6 7 4	5 5 6 6 7
6 6 7 8 9	6 9 8 7 7
6 7 7 8 1	6 7 8 9 9

Each of the above hands, or cribs, reckons sixteen points. In these examples we see how effective a number of low cards are—such as Aces, Twos and Threes,—when grouped together. We also see those telling combinations produced by an association of Fours, Fives and Sixes; as well as Sevens, Eights and Nines.

Sixteen may also be formed with Tenth cards exclusively, thus:— two Kings, two Queens, and any Knave that is not of the same suit as the start card.

Or, two Tens, two Knaves, and a Queen;

Or, two Queens, two Tens and a Knave;

Or, two Knaves, two Queens and a King.

In every instance—the Knave that is employed to form a sixteen hand—must be of a suit differing from that of the start cards—unless the Knave is turned for the start. (See " *Fifth Question,*).

Sixteen may also be made with Tenth cards as follows: One King, three Queens, and a Knave of the same suit as the start card.

Any three Tenth cards with any other two Tenth cards, that will form sequences, will produce this result, provided—the Knave is of the same suit as the start-card.

The Number Fifteen may be produced as follows:—

1	1	1	2	3		1	2	3	3	3
1	3	3	3	2		2	2	2	3	4

Fifteen may also be composed of Tenth cards, thus:—three Tens, a Knave and a Queen, provided the Knave, if held in hand, is *not* of the same suit as the start-card; because if it were, it would make sixteen instead of fifteen. The following combination also yields fifteen :— A sequence of Eight, Seven, Six and Five of the same suit, and the Two of the same suit for the start-card.

The Number Fourteen is produced in a variety of ways; we give here some examples.

1	2	2	3	10		1	2	3	3	9
1	6	6	7	8		2	6	6	7	8
3	3	4	5	6		3	3	6	6	9
3	3	4	5	7		3	4	4	5	6
3	3	9	9	9		4	5	6	6	7
3	4	5	5	6		5	5	5	1	10
3	3	4	5	8		5	6	7	8	8
4	4	7	7	7		5	6	7	7	8
8	7	6	6	1		8	8	7	7	1

Fourteen may also be obtained by any of the following *flush* sequences:—

4 5 6 7 8   2 3 4 5 6
5 6 7 8 9   6 7 8 9 10

and by the following combinations:—

Eight, Seven, Six, Five of the same suit, with the Two of another suit for the start-card.

A flush of Knave, Five, Four, Three, Two; any card except the Knave being the start-card.

A flush of Knave, Nine, Eight, Seven, Six; the Knave *not* being the start-card.

The Number Thirteen seldom occurs, but may be obtained in the following ways:

A sequence of Six, Seven, Eight and a pair of Aces.

A pair-royal of Threes, and a Knave in hand, with a Two for the start-card, of the same suit as the Knave.

Three Knaves and a Two (or two Knaves and two Twos,) with a Three turned up of the same suit as either of the Knaves.

Two, Three, Four, Five, and any Tenth card except the Knave, all being of the same suit.

Knave, Ten, Nine, Eight and Seven, all of a suit, the Knave *not* being the start-card.

Seven, Six, Five, Four, all of a suit, and the Eight of another suit turned up.

The Number Twelve is obtained by a great many combinations. Thus:

1	1	1	3	10		1	1	1	5	8
1	1	1	6	7		1	1	4	4	10
2	2	2	4	7		2	2	2	5	6
2	2	2	6	7		2	2	2	3	8
3	3	3	5	7		3	3	3	4	8
4	4	4	6	1		5	6	6	7	2
5	5	7	7	3		5	6	6	7	9
5	6	6	7	8		5	7	7	6	3
7	7	7	3	5		6	6	6	1	8
8	8	8	5	2		6	6	6	1	2
8	7	6	6	3		7	6	6	6	2
8	8	8	6	1		7	7	1	1	8
9	9	9	1	5		7	7	7	6	2
					8	8	8	4	3	

Twelve may also be produced by the rare occurrence of a double pair-royal, four cards of the same denomination, provided the remaining card will not make any fifteens.

The Number Eleven does not occur very often. It is produced by some combination similar *to* two Sixes, a Seven, and an Eight, with a Knave of the same suit as the start-card.

It may also consist of a full five flush sequence, in which no fifteens occur, but containing the Knave in the hand.

The Number Ten is formed by a double sequence of small cards, thus :—

1	1	2	3	4		1	2	2	3	4
1	2	3	3	4		1	2	3	4	4

The Number Nine is usually produced by a sequence of five cards containing two fifteens, thus:—

Four, Five, Six, Seven, Eight;

Five, Six, Seven, Eight, Nine,

Six, Seven, Eight, Nine, Ten.

Nine is also formed by a sequence of cards in which no fifteen occurs, the four cards held in hand being of the same suit, but the start-card of a different suit, thus :—

Eight, Nine, Ten, Knave in suit, with any other Queen;

Or, Nine, Ten, Knave, Queen in suit, with another King.

Nine will also occur when the five cards contain a triplet, and a pair, from which no fifteens can be made, and provided one of these consists of Knaves, and one of the Knaves can count " one for his nob."

The Number Eight may be formed in several ways. From Knave, One, Two, Three and Four, provided the Knave is the start-card; or, if in the hand, of a different suit from the start-card.

Or, from Knave and any other Tenth card, with Three, Four, Five, (or Five, Six, Seven), provided the Knave is in hand and of the same suit as the start-card.

Or, any pair of Tenth cards, and another Tenth card, with Two and Three (or One and Four).

The combination formed by three cards of the same denomination (or pair-royal), with a pair will amount to eight points, provided none of the cards will combine to make fifteens. Thus three Aces with any pair, except Sixes or Sevens, will count eight points. Three Twos, with any pair except Nines; three Threes with any pair except Sixes or Nines; three Fours with any pair except Sevens, etc., will each make eight points.

The pairs which form the exceptions are excluded because they make fifteens, raising the value of the hand to ten, twelve or fourteen points, as the case may be, besides nine combinations of a pair-royal with a pair which count twenty points each.

The Number Seven will result from a straight sequence of five cards, not in suit, containing one fifteen; either One, Two, Three, Four, Five ; or, Seven, Eight, Nine, Ten, Knave ; the Knave being the start-card ; or, if in hand, of different suit from the start-card.

Seven will also result from a flush of five cards, not in sequence, and containing one fifteen.

Also, from cards containing two fifteens and a sequence of three, such as, One, Two, Three, Nine, Ten; or, Two, Three, Four, Eight, Ten. There are numerous combinations of four cards which may make seven, but very few which involve all of the five cards, and are generally too simple to require special mention.

In all the foregoing combinations, as has already been stated, all the five cards are considered necessary to produce the points given, but they embrace all the prominent combinations, and explain those which at first sight might be obscure or eccentric.

FIVE-CARD CRIBBAGE.

In playing Five-card Cribbage, the object and method of playing the game is, in the main, the same as in the Six-card game, and the same laws apply to both.

There are, however, some notable points of difference, arising from the nature of the preliminary conditions, and the consequent changes necessary to comply with them.

It will be understood that, excepting in the cases noted below, all the arrangements and rules of the Fix-card game remain in force.

In dealing the cards the dealer gives each player alternately, one by one, five cards.

Each player discards two for the dealer's crib, retaining three cards in hand.

The non-dealer, at the commencement of the game, is allowed to mark three holes at any time, as an offset to the advantage of the first deal. This is technically known as " three for last;" it is usually best to mark these three points at once, to avoid omission or possible dispute.

As soon as a " go," or thirty-one is reached, the remaining cards in the hands (if any), are not played.

Five-card cribbage is considered more scientific than the six-card game; the opportunities for marking, both in play and in the hand, being so much less, every point is of value, a single point gained or lost frequently deciding the game.

Skillful players, therefore, consider it important to play for the "go," which makes or loses a point, and is equivalent to a gain of two points to the player making it. To this end it is best, as a general rule, with two low cards and a high one, to commence with a low card; with two high cards and a low one, to begin with a high one. The dealer's chance of making the "go" is greater than that of the non-dealer.

At Five-card Cribbage it is, as a rule, more important to lay out bad cards for the adversary's crib (called *baulking the crib*), than to keep the cards in hand which will give you the greatest score; for the crib and start together consist of five cards, the hand and start of only four cards.

The largest number, with but very few exceptions, that can be made out of four cards is twelve; but, with five cards, there are many hands that score from twelve to twenty-nine. Hence it is advisable to put out for the opponent's crib the most unlikely scoring cards.

Moreover, if your adversary is a good player, he will for the most part prefer the interest of his crib to that of his hand. Hence he will put out cards that are likely to make long scores in combination with three others; and this is an additional reason for baulking his crib.

In order to know whether you should play on or play off (see Hint No. 10), you must keep in mind that the average points in the play of the hand are two for the dealer, and one-and-a-half for the non-dealer; that the average points in hand are more than four and less than five; and that the average points in crib are five. Each player ought, therefore, to make six in hand and play throughout the game, and seventeen-and-a-half in two deals.

If the players score this average, they are said to be *at home.*

If you score the average or more, and leave your adversary about seven holes in arrear, you are said to be *safe at home.*

When you are at home you should play off; when your adversary is safe at home you should play on.

The rule given in Hint No. 3, page 23, in regard to sequences, is not always applicable, when you are *safe at home.* It is ad visible to be able to "play off" with a card which will not work in with the sequence.

But, when near the end of the game, sequences should be encouraged, in order to play out.

AN INSTRUCTIVE FIVE-CARD EXAMPLE.

The vicissitudes of Cribbage are so great that a player need never despair of the game, whatever may be the disparity in the score.

For instance: A and B are playing five-card Cribbage ; B has already scored fifty-six, while A has not made a single point.

A deals, and gives B a Six, two Sevens, a Four and a Three, while he deals himself three Sixes, with a Three and a Two.

B, if a good player, would lay out his Four and Three, and hold his Six and two Sevens in hand.

A, playing well, must discard his Three and Two, and hold his pair-royal of Sixes.

The *start* or turn-up card is a Three.

B begins by playing one of his Sevens; A follows with a Six, making thirteen; then B pairs A's Sis, calling nineteen, and scoring two for the pair, which makes him within three holes of game. A then plays another Six, making twenty-five, and a pair-royal, for which he takes six, and as B is not able to come in with his remaining Seven, A adds his other Six, making thirty-one, and a double pair-royal, for all of which he marks fourteen points more.

B then takes two points for his hand, which makes him within one of game.

A marks twelve for his hand, which makes him thirty-two holes (having played twenty). A next marks seventeen points for his crib, which makes him in all forty-nine points.

B then deals, and gives A the Three of Hearts, the Four of Hearts, and the Five of Hearts, with any two tenth cards. B gives himself a Seven, Eight, Nine, Queen and King.

A, playing well, lays out his two tenth cards, and holds his Three, Four, and Five of Hearts.

B, to play correctly, lays out his King and Queen, and remains with his Seven, Eight, and Nine.

The start card is Three.

A then leads off his Four, and B follows with an Eight, making twelve. A replies with his Three, making fifteen, and scores two, while B fellows with his Nine, making twenty-four. A then comes in with his Five, forming twenty-nine, and marks one for the end hole, as B is not able to bring in his last card.

A then marks thirteen points for his hand, which is four points more than he wants, and remains the conqueror.

The above example is worthy of the attention of the faint-hearted votary of Cribbage, and to be appreciated it should be played over with the cards. It is both interesting and instructive ; as, at every stage of the game both parties invariably make the best possible play according to their cards.

THREE-HANDED CRIBBAGE.

The game of Three-handed Cribbage is not often practised. It is played, as its name imports, by three persons; the board is of a triangular shape, containing three sets of holes of sixty each, with the sixty-first or game-hole.

Each of the three players is furnished separately with pegs, and scores his game in the usual manner.

Three-handed Cribbage is subject to the same laws as the other varieties of the game.

The calculations as to discarding and playing are very similar; but it must be remembered that as all three are independent, you have two antagonists instead of one.

Five cards compose the deal. They are dealt one at a time, and after dealing the fifteenth, another, or sixteenth card, is dealt face downwards from the pack, to constitute the foundation of the crib. To this each of the three players by discarding adds one card, and the crib, therefore, consists of four cards, while each individual remains with four cards in hand.

The deal and crib are originally cut for, and afterwards pass alternately.

It is obvious that you will be still even, if you gain only one game out of three, since the winner receives a double stake, which is furnished by the two losers to him who first attains the sixty-first hole.

It has been computed that he who has the second deal has rather the best chance of victory; but there seems very little difference.

FOUR-HANDED CRIBBAGE.

The game of Four-handed Cribbage is played by four persons, in partnerships of two and two, as at Whist—each sitting opposite to his partner. Sixty-one points constitute the game; but it is usual to go twice round the board, making the game one hundred and twenty-one.

At the commencement of the sitting, it is decided which two of the four players shall have the management of the score, and the board is placed between them. The other two are not allowed to touch the board or pegs, though each may prompt his partner, and point out any omissions or irregularities he may discover in computation or scoring. The laws which govern Six-card Cribbage are equally applicable here.

It is the usual custom to play rubbers, and to cut for partners every rubber. The two highest and two lowest play together. The Ace is always lowest. If it is decided not to change partners after a game or rubber, there must still be a fresh cut for the deal. Each may shuffle the cards in turn according to the laws which regulate this operation at Whist.

The deal and crib pass round the table in rotation to the left. The usual laws of Cribbage regulate the act of dealing, as to exposing cards, and so forth; and no one is suffered to touch his hand until the deal is complete. Before dealing, the cards must be cut by the player on the *right-hand* of the dealer.

The dealer gives to each player in rotation one card at a time, beginning with the player to his left, until all have received five cards. The remainder of the pack he places on his left hand. Each person then lays out one card for the crib, which is, of course, the property of the dealer. The left-hand adversary must discard first, and so round the table; the dealer laying out last. There is no advantage in this, but such is the custom.

As there is but one card to be laid out from the five received by each player, there is seldom much difficulty in making the choice. Fives are the best cards to give your own crib, and you will never, therefore, give them to your antagonists. Low cards are generally best for the crib, and Kings or Aces the worst. Aces sometimes tell to great advantage in the play at this game.

When your partner has to deal, the crib, being equally your own, must be favored in the same way. Before discarding, always consider with whom the deal stands.

When all have discarded for the crib, the pack is cut for the start-card. This cut is made by the player to the *left* of the dealer lifting the pack, when the dealer takes off the top card and places it face upwards upon the pack. Observe, that the dealer's *right-hand* adversary cuts before dealing, but his *left-hand* adversary cuts for the start-card.

Having cut the start-card, the player on the left-hand of the dealer leads off first, the next player to the left following, and so on round the table, till the whole of the sixteen cards are played out according to the laws.

Fifteens, sequences, pairs, &c, reckon in the usual way for those who obtain them.

Should either player be unable to come in under thirty-one, he declares it to be a *go,* and the right of play devolves on his left-hand neighbor.

No small cards must be kept in band which would come in under a penalty. Thus, should A play an Ace, making the number twenty-eight, and should each of the other three pass it without playing, not having cards low enough to come in—on its coming round to A, be must play if he can under thirty-one, whether he gain any additional points by so doing or not. Example :

B plays an Ace and makes thirty. Neither of the other three can come in, and on the turn to play coming round again to B, he plays another Ace, and marks four points: two for the pair of Aces, and two for the thirty-one.

Many similar examples might be adduced, and there frequently arise complicated cases of sequences made this way out of low cards. *(See* Long sequences in Four-handed Cribbage, page 59). Indeed, the playing out of the hand requires much more watchfulness than in Two-handed Cribbage. So many points are made by play in Four-handed Cribbage that it is essential to play as much as possible to the points, or stages, of the game.

When the hand is played out, the amount of each hand is pegged, the crib being taken last. He who led off must score first, and so on round to the dealer. Each calls the number to which he considers himself entitled, and watches to see that they are scored properly; while at the same time he does not fail to scan his adversaries' cards with an observant eye to see that they do not take more than their due.

Tho amount of points to be expected, on an average, from each hand, is seven, and from the crib about four to five.

From the play, it is computed that each of the four players should average five points every time. Reasoning on these data, the non-dealers are at home, at the close of the first round, should they have obtained nineteen or twenty points: and the dealers are at home at the end of the first round should they have acquired twenty-three or twenty-four.

At the finish of the second round, with their average number, each set of players would be forty-two to forty-three. At the close of the third round, the non-dealers should be just out, or else the dealers are likely to win, being the non-dealers in the next round.

There is no advantage in having the deal, the chances are so various that the parties start fully equal, no matter whether with, or without the deal.

From the above calculation, the game going only once round the board, should be over in three rounds. Those who have *not* the first deal, have the original chance of winning, *if they can keep it,* holding average cards throughout the game. Should they fail in making this good, those who dealt at the commencement of the game will generally sweep all, having had their second crib, and first show afterwards.

The non-dealers should observe moderato caution in the first hand, but under this head it is needless to say more to either party, than to impress it upon them again and again, to become thoroughly acquainted with the number, of points which form medium hands, to keep a close watch on the state of the game, and play accordingly.

HINTS ON PLAYING FOUR-HANDED CRIBBAGE.

In leading off, great care is necessary. A Five is a had lead, because the chances of a Tenth card are so numerous. An Ace is not a good lead, as a Tenth card paired makes it twenty-one. A Nine is a bad lead because the Six (to make fifteen), if paired by your partner, makes twenty-one. Threes and Pours are the safest.

Pair cards with caution, weighing well the chances of a pair-royal against you; as second player, make *fifteen* in preference to a pair, if both are possible.

When nearly out, keep Aces and low cards for play. When playing *off,* avoid risk of sequences; when playing *on,* make or invite them.

As third player, play below twenty-one if you can, to give your partner the chance of the *go,* or of making the two points for thirty-one.

Holding Aces, it is frequently better play, when you have the option, to make twenty-seven or twenty-eight, than thirty, in order to have a chance of bringing in your Aces, which sometimes yield a heavy amount of points at that stage of the computation.

LONG SEQUENCES IN FOUR-HANDED CRIBBAGE.

In a four-handed game, the formation of sequences during the play of the hands sometimes occasions doubt as to their correctness and consequent dispute.

The fundamental principle on which such sequences are founded is that they must be formed by cards in the exact order or *rotation* in which they are played, always counting backwards from the last card played.

Disputes can always be easily and definitely decided by laying the cards in a straight line, each player, in his proper turn, placing his card in rotation on the line.

As an illustration of this, we give an example:—

A, B, C and D are playing a four-handed game at Cribbage;

> A commences and plays a Six;
> B follows with a Five;
> C plays a Four.

The cards now displayed, if placed in a line in rotation as they are played, and counting backwards from the last card played, are

4 5 6

making a three-sequence for C to score.

D now plays a Three. The rotation of the cards is now (always counting backwards)

3 4 5 6

making a four-sequence for D to score.

A, beginning a second round, plays a Six. The rotation of cards, backwards, is now

6 3 4 5 6

making a four-sequence for A; the Six first played being of no further value.

B, having no card in his hand which will come in without exceeding a card-count of thirty-one, says "go."

C now plays a Four. The cards played so far, counting backwards in the rotation *in which they fell* will show

4 6 3 4

making no sequence.

It is worthy of notice that, if the cards played were laid in front of each player in the regular way, thus:—

6

3   **5**

4

B's Five would still be visible (because he was unable to play to the second round), and would at first sight *appear* to come in for a sequence.

But this would violate the fundamental rule of sequences; B's Five was the *second* card played, and cannot be reckoned or brought in between the *sixth and fifth* cards played; it is not in direct rotation of play, the actual fall of the cards, counting backwards from the last one played, would be thus:—

4 6 3 4 5 6

resulting in 4, 6, 3 and the next 4 barring any sequence.

A REMARKABLE PROBLEM IN FOUR-HANDED CRIBBAGE.

The following possible combination of hands in a four-handed game at Cribbage, shows how two partners having the deal may score sixty-one points merely in the play of their cards, without holding a single point in their hands, and without the aid of their "crib."

Suppose A and C are partners, and playing against B and D.

A is dealer, and deals to each hand a Three, Four, Six, Seven, and one Tenth card.

Each player discards his Tenth card, and neither of them has a single point in his hand to score.

D, the right-hand opponent of the dealer A cuts a Knave (also known as a *Jack*) for the start card.

The play and score of each partnership will be as follows:—

	A & C.	B & D.
A, the dealer scores "two for his heels."	2	
B, eldest hand, leads a Three.		
C, follows with his Three and scores a pair...........................	2	
D, plays his Three and scores a triple-pair...........................		6
A's Three then scores a Pair-Royal..	12	
B next leads his Four.		
C follows with his Four and pairs....	2	
D plays his Four and scores a triple..		6
A makes with his Four a Pair-Royal	12	
and one peg additional for the "go"	1	
B now leads his Seven, and in playing this round the partners make the same score as in the preceding round............................	15	6
B finally leads his Six, with the same results, which bring A and C's score	15	6
up to a grand total of sixty-one	——	——
points against their opponents'	61	24

twenty-four. Thus A and C win the game in one hand, without holding a single point to score from the count of their hands, or making any use of their "crib."

LAWS OF CRIBBAGE.

CUTTING.

1. A cut must consist of at least four cards. In cutting for deal, the player cutting first must leave sufficient cards for the player cutting last to make a legal cut. He who cuts last must not leave less than four cards in the remainder of the pack.

2. The player who cuts the lowest Cribbage card deals. The Ace is lowest. The other cards rank in sequence order, as at Whist, the King being highest.

3. If, in cutting for deal, a player exposes more than one card, his adversary may treat whichever of the exposed cards he pleases as the one cut.

4. If, in cutting to the dealer, a card is exposed; or, if, in re-uniting the separated packets the dealer expose a card; or there is any confusion of the cards, there must be a fresh cut.

5. There must be a fresh cut for deal after each game, unless rubbers are played.

SHUFFLING AND DEALING.

6. Each player has a right to shuffle the cards. • The dealer has the right to shuffle last. The players deal alternately throughout the game.

7. The dealer must deal the cards by one at a time to each player, commencing with his adversary. If he deals two together, he may rectify the error, provided he can do so by moving one card only; otherwise, there must be a fresh deal, and the non-dealer marks two holes.

8. If the dealer exposes any of his own cards, there is no penalty. If he exposes one of his adversary's, the adversary marks two holes, and has the option of a fresh deal, *prior to* looking at his hand. If a card is exposed through the non-dealer's fault, the dealer marks two, and has the option of dealing again.

9. If it is discovered while dealing that there is a faced card in the pack, there must be a fresh deal, without penalty.

10. If the dealer gives his adversary or himself too many cards, the non-dealer marks two holes, and a fresh deal ensues; but, in such case, the non-dealer must discover the error before he takes up his cards, or he cannot claim the two, though there must still be a new deal. The deal never passes, as it does in Whist, by way of penalty, but the dealer deals over again.

11. If the dealer gives his adversary or himself too few cards, the non-dealer marks two holes, and has the option, *after* looking at his hand, of a fresh deal, or of allowing the imperfect hand to be completed from the top of the pack.

12. If a player deals out of turn, and the error is discovered before the start is turned up, the deal in error is void, and the right dealer deals. After the start is turned up, it is too late to rectify the error.

LAYING OUT.

13. If either player lays out when he holds too many cards, the adversary marks two holes, and has the option of a fresh deal, or of standing the deal. If he stands the deal, he has the right of drawing the surplus card or cards from the offender's hand, and of looking at them.

14. If either player lays out with too few cards in hand, he must play out the hand with less than the right number of cards.

15. The dealer may insist on his adversary's laying out first. In the Three or Four-handed game each must lay out in rotation, the dealer last.

16. If a player takes back into his hand a card he has laid out, his adversary makes two holes, and has the option of a fresh deal.

17. The crib must not be touched during the play of the hand.

18. In cutting for the start, the non-dealer must cut at least four cards, and must leave at least four cards in the lower packet.

19. If the dealer turns up more than one card, the non-dealer or eldest hand may choose which of the exposed cards shall be the start.

20. If a Knave is turned up, and the dealer has played his first card without scoring his heels, he forfeits the two points.

PLAYING.

21. If a player plays with too many cards in hand, his adversary marks two holes, and has the option of a fresh deal. If he elects to stand the deal, he has the right of drawing the surplus card or cards from the offender's hand, and of looking at them, and the option of playing the hand again, or not.

22. If a player plays with too few cards, there is no penalty.

23. If a card that will come in is played, it cannot be taken up again. If a card that will not come in is played, no penalty attaches to the exposure.

24. If two cards are played together, the card counted is deemed to be the one played, and the other must be taken back into the player's hand.

25. If a player neglects to play when he has a card that will come in, his opponent may require it to be played, or may mark two holes. (This rule does not apply to the player who has the " go " at two-handed Five-card Cribbage.)

26. There is no penalty for miscounting during the play.

SHOWING AND SCORING.

27. When reckoning a hand or crib, the cards must be plainly shown, and must remain exposed until the opponent is satisfied as to the nature of the claim.

28. If a player mixes his hand or crib with each other, or with the pack, before his claim is properly made {see Law 27), he forfeits any score the hand or crib may contain.

29. If a player scores more points than he is entitled to, the adversary marks backwards, off the offender's score the excess of points wrongfully taken and adds the same number to his own score. This law applies even if a player, in consequence of over-scoring, places his foremost peg in the game-hole.

30. There is no penalty for scoring too few points. A player is not bound to assist his adversary in making out his score.

31. When a peg is quitted the score cannot be altered, except as provided in Law 29.

32. If a player touches his opponent's pegs (except to put back an over-score), or, if he touches his own pegs, except when he has a score to make, his adversary marks two holes.

33. If a player displaces his foremost peg, he must put it behind the other. If he displaces both his pegs, his adversary is entitled to place the hindmost peg where he believes it to have been, and the other peg must then be put behind it.

34. A lurch (or double game), cannot be claimed, unless by previous agreement.

35. The "three for last" (at Five-card Cribbage) may be scored at any time during the game, but not after the opponent has scored sixty-one.

The foregoing Laws are derived, from the best authorities on Cribbage, and have been carefully revised to conform with the latest usages that have been adopted in playing the game.

The general and special directions for the guidance of players, which are introduced in their proper connections, are designed to provide for and fully answer the questions which so often arise from a want of thorough familiarity with the points at issue, and are often sufficiently embarrassing; this is especially the case in long sequences in play, as distinguished from sequences in the hand.

The great variety of combinations which occur in Cribbage, demands a thorough knowledge of all the intricacies of the game, the want of which causes frequent disputes; but a careful study of the explanations given on every difficult point should be sufficient to clear up and provide for all contingencies that might otherwise appear doubtful.

55451109R00032

Made in the USA
Lexington, KY
23 September 2016